SUGAR ART
Ideas

FANCY EGGS

SUGAR ART
Ideas

FANCY EGGS

MARY VERGHESE

Consultant: NICHOLAS LODGE
Series Editor: ALISON LEACH

MEREHURST PRESS
LONDON

I dedicate this book to my husband Joe and my children, George and Miriam without whose love, help and understanding I would not have written this book.

My special thanks to Tombi Peck, Nicholas Lodge, Jan Clarke, Joan Abreu, Jenny, Gay and all the staff at B.R. Mathews and all my friends for their support.

Published 1989 by Merehurst Press
Ferry House, 51-57 Lacy Road, Putney
London SW15 1PR

Co-published in Australia and New Zealand by Child & Associates,
Unit C, 5 Skyline Place, Frenchs Forest, 2086, Australia.

© Copyright 1989 Merehurst Limited

ISBN 1 85391 049 X

Managing Editor: Alison Leach
Designer: Richard Slater
Photographer: Graham Tann, assisted by Alister Thorpe, Lucy Baker and Gary Taylor
Typeset by Vision Typesetting, Manchester
Colour separation by Scantrans Pte Limited, Singapore
Printed in Belgium by Proost International Book Production

Warning
Cocktail sticks and wired flowers must only be used for display purposes in sugarcraft. Great care should always be taken to ensure there is no possibility of any particles being eaten accidentally.

Important: use only one set of measurements. The quantities given in metric are not always exact conversions of the imperial measurements. Cup conversions of imperial measurements of ingredients mentioned in this book are given below.

Imperial	Cups
1lb caster (superfine) sugar	2 cups
1lb icing (confectioner's) suger	$3\frac{1}{2}$ cups

CONTENTS

FOREWORD

This fascinating book is about a very unusual aspect of sugarcraft, with everything being made from a basic egg shape. We tend to think only of chocolate Easter eggs, but in this book you will find lots of ideas for many other occasions.

I first met Mary Verghese just over three years ago when she attended a class that I was giving at B.R. Mathews, the sugarcraft specialist shop in London. I very soon realized that Mary was an exceptional person, both in her dedication to sugarcraft and in her wonderful personality. She continued to attend my classes and we became friends. One day she told me about her other hobbies including eggcraft. I asked her to bring some examples of her work to the next class. The eggs were beautiful.

Earlier this year when the idea of doing an eggcraft book was suggested at a planning meeting with the publishers, I thought it would work very well and knew immediately who should write it. After a telephone call to Mary, she agreed to be the author.

I am sure that once you have read through this book, you will agree it is full of wonderful ideas.

I wish Mary the very best of everything with this book which will be an asset for everyone interested in sugar- or eggcraft.

Nicholas Lodge

INTRODUCTION

About ten years ago I bought a book on decorating eggs in a shop in India as I was fascinated by what could be achieved using an ordinary egg shell.

However, my interest in the subject went no further until 1984 when I was living in England. I decided to go to evening classes in cake decorating at my local adult education centre. I was delighted to discover the following year that they also ran a course on egg decorating which I eagerly joined. After a couple of terms I realized how well my two interests combined.

Through the ages people have believed that the egg has certain mystic powers and numerous legends exist from pagan times. To the ancient philosopher the egg symbolized the four elements of earth, air, water and fire.

The Druids considered the egg to be sacred and were not therefore allowed to eat it. An egg shape in the form of a locket worn round the neck was a symbol of rank.

In the Christian religion the egg represents rebirth and resurrection. The custom of giving Easter eggs is derived from this belief.

The people of ancient Persia (Iran) gave each other eggs dyed red to celebrate the first day of spring. The Chinese gave eggs to the parents of new-born babies.

The early German settlers, later known as the Pennsylvanian Dutch, introduced the craft of decorated eggs to America. The egg tree is said to have originated from them; nowadays a tree or branch decorated with eggs is very common in many parts of America at Easter.

The Mexicans use blown eggs filled with confetti to celebrate the New Year. In Poland Easter eggs are covered with wax in which a design is scratched and then dyed with vegetable dyes. When the wax is melted, the design is left on the egg.

A President's wife brought the Easter game of egg-rolling to the United States. Originally children rolled eggs down Capitol Hill but now the game is played on the White House lawns each year.

It is of course the exquisite jewelled eggs of the renowned Carl Fabergé that are the best source of inspiration in developing new ideas.

Mary Verghese

RECIPES

Caster sugar mixture

600g (1¼lb) caster (superfine) sugar
about 30ml (2 tbsp) water

Mix the sugar and water together with a spoon until it resembles wet sand. To test if the mixture is the correct consistency, press your finger or the back of the spoon into the sugar. If the imprint remains, then it is correct. Otherwise add a little more water.

If you want to make coloured eggs, colour the water before you mix it with the sugar. Make sure that you have enough mixture for whatever you are going to make because it is difficult to match the shade again exactly. Make the colour slightly darker than you need because it dries lighter and by the time you have scooped out the inside of the egg, it will be lighter still.

Moulding paste

225g (8oz) mallow Russe
20ml (4 tsp) skimmed milk
10ml (2 tsp) white vegetable fat
450g (1lb) icing (confectioner's) sugar
40ml (8 tsp) cornflour (cornstarch)
15ml (1 tbsp) gum tragacanth

Place the mallow Russe, skimmed milk and vegetable fat in a double boiler and dissolve over a gentle heat. Do not let the mixture boil. Alternatively, you can use a microwave for a minute.

Sift the icing sugar, cornflour and gum tragacanth into a mixer bowl. Add the dissolved mallow Russe mixture and beat thoroughly.

Sprinkle some icing sugar on a work surface and knead the mixture until it is no longer sticky. The more you knead it, the whiter it will become.

Store the paste in a plastic bag in an air-tight container. It is best if left overnight but in an emergency it can be used as soon as it has cooled. Items made with this paste take a day or two to become really hard. This enables you to work on them in the meantime, neatening the edges of moulds and cutting out windows, for instance.

Pastillage gum paste

40ml (8 tsp) cold water
7.5ml (1½ tsp) powdered
  gelatine
450g (1lb) icing (confectioner's)
  sugar
2.5ml (½ tsp) gum tragacanth

Pour the water into a heatproof jug, sprinkle the gelatine on top and stand for 1 hour.

Sift the icing sugar into an ovenproof bowl. Add the gum tragacanth and warm the sugar by placing the bowl in a very cool oven for about 45 minutes. If the icing sugar is cold, the gelatine may set in spots.

Completely dissolve the gelatine over hot, not boiling, water or place in the microwave on high power for 30 seconds, checking after 15 seconds. Do not let it boil.

Pour the dissolved gelatine into the warmed icing sugar, stirring with a warmed spoon. Then knead until the mixture forms a smooth stiff paste.

Store the mixture in a plastic bag inside an air-tight container and leave for at least 24 hours to mature before using.

When using this paste, dust the work surface with cornflour (cornstarch), but care

should be taken not to use too much as this would make the paste too dry, causing it to crack while working with it. This paste can be used for modelling animals, bells, cribs and other small figures.

Flower paste

25ml (5 tsp) cold water
10ml (2 tsp) powdered gelatine
450g (1lb) icing (confectioner's)
  sugar
15ml (1 tbsp) gum tragacanth
20ml (4 tsp) white vegetable fat
10ml (2 tsp) liquid glucose
1 large egg white, string
  removed

Pour the water into a heatproof jug, sprinkle the gelatine on top and stand for 1 hour.

Sift the icing sugar into an ovenproof container, ideally a large stainless steel mixer bowl. Add the gum tragacanth to the icing sugar. Warm the sugar by placing the bowl in a very cool oven for about 45 minutes.

Completely dissolve the gelatine over hot, not boiling water, or place in the microwave on high power for 30 seconds, checking it after 15 seconds. Do not let it boil. When the gelatine has completely dissolved, add the liquid glucose and white vegetable fat and heat till melted.

Remove the sugar mixture from the oven, return the bowl to the mixer and fix the warmed beater in place. Add the gelatine mixture and the egg white to the bowl and turn on at the lowest speed. Mix gently until the ingredients are combined and the mixture is

off-white in colour. Then turn the mixer to maximum speed and beat till the mixture is stringy and whiter. This may take 1–5 minutes depending on your mixer.

Store the paste in a plastic bag in an air-tight container and leave in the refrigerator for 24 hours to mature.

When using this paste, work a small piece in your hand. The warmth of your hand will make the paste pliable and of the consistency of chewing gum. If the paste is dry and crumbly, add a tiny bit of egg white and white vegetable fat, and work till the correct texture.

This paste is particularly good for fine work and for flowers, such as those used on the Pansy Egg (*see page 17*).

BASIC EGG MOULDING

Moulding eggs in caster sugar

For one 14-cm (5½-in) egg you will need about 600g (1¼lb) caster sugar mixture (*see page 8*).

1 Press the caster sugar mixture into an egg mould, using the back of a spoon to eliminate any air pockets. When the mould is tightly packed, slide a spatula along the top to level it. Then turn the egg out on to a flat surface Repeat the process for the other half. Leave for about 3–4 hours, until the egg halves are dry enough to hold.
   Using a spoon, scoop out the insides of each half which will still be soft.
   Stick both halves of the egg together with a little royal icing. Cover the join with a shell border or with a ribbon.

2 To make a window in the front of a caster sugar egg, hold a piece of damp cotton taut and slide this along the top of the egg as soon as you have turned it out on to the flat surface. Leave to dry before removing the top and scooping out the inside of the egg.

Moulding eggs in paste

For one 14-cm (5½-in) egg you will need 450g (1lb) moulding paste (*see page 8*).

1 Knead the paste until it is smooth. Divide in two equal portions. Roll out one portion of the paste to 3–6-mm (⅛–¼-in) thick, depending on how you intend to use the finished egg. Repeat the process with the other portion.

Dust the moulds and the rolled-out paste lightly with cornflour (cornstarch). Ease one portion of the paste, the cornflour-dusted side outwards, into an egg mould, pressing it gently to make sure it fits closely. Trim off the excess paste using a sharp knife with a flexible blade. Repeat with the remaining paste for the other half of the egg.

Leave in the moulds to dry for about 6–8 hours. Then turn the eggs out on to a flat surface and leave until completely dry, preferably overnight or even longer depending on the thickness of the eggs.

2 To make a window in the front of a paste egg, hold a template of the required shape in the base of the mould with your fingertips, and cut through the paste round the edge with a scalpel. When the egg is dry and turned out on to a flat surface, the cut-out can be removed easily.

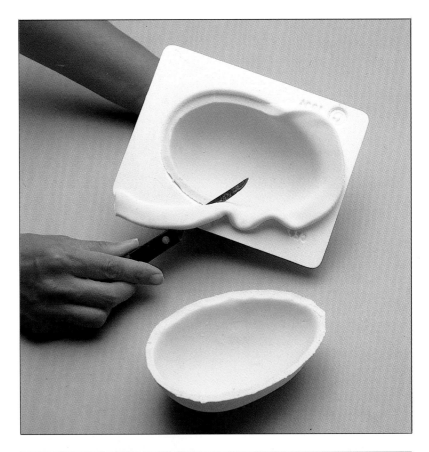

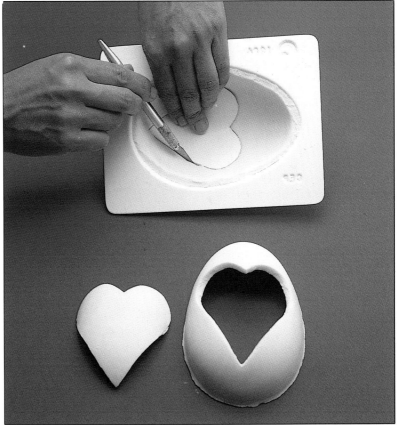

STANDS FOR EGGS

Some of the more elaborate eggs in this book are displayed on stands, which can be in the shape of candlesticks or flat plaques. The stands can be sprayed with food colouring, painted with non-edible gold colouring or piped with tiny blossoms in complementary shades.

Basic stand

1 Roll some moulding paste (*see page 8*) into a tube about 12-mm ($\frac{1}{2}$-in) in diameter and 6-cm ($2\frac{1}{2}$-in) long. To give the stand strength, insert a cocktail stick (toothpick) through the centre of the tube. Indent one end of the tube and place it on a piece of foam sponge so that it dries in a round shape rather than having a flat side.

2 Roll out some moulding paste and cut out a circle about 5-cm (2-in) in diameter. Scallop the edge with a crimper and place in a plastic apple tray (such as used by supermarkets) to cup it slightly. Roll out another circle a little larger than the first and crimp the edge. Leave to dry flat.

3 Attach the cupped circle to the indented end of the tube with royal icing. Attach the flat circle to form the base of the stand.

4 When completely dry, paint gold or silver with non-edible colouring. If the stands are not being eaten, you could use an aerosol paint spray to obtain an even metallic finish.

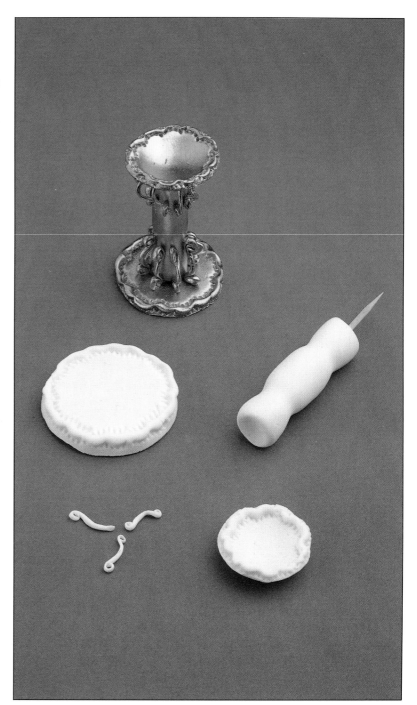

Decorated basic stand

1 Roll some moulding paste (*see page 8*) into a tube about 12-mm ($\frac{1}{2}$-in) in diameter and 5-cm (2-in) long. Shape the tube by rolling your little finger across it 12-mm ($\frac{1}{2}$-in) from the top and 12-mm ($\frac{1}{2}$-in) from the bottom.

2 Roll out tiny balls of moulding paste into thin strings. Curl both ends of each piece and stick to the sides of the shaped tube. Make at least eleven curly strings for the base. Then roll out more tiny balls of moulding paste into thin strings, but this time only curl one end of each piece. Stick the other end under the cupped circle on the top of the tube. When dry, paint with non-edible gold colouring or any desired food colouring.

Petunia stand

1 Using the middle-sized petunia cutter, cut out two petunia shapes in moulding paste (*see page 8*). Dry one flat and the other in an apple tray to cup it slightly. Using the smallest petunia cutter, cut one petunia shape and dry flat.

2 Roll some moulding paste into a tube about 12-mm ($\frac{1}{2}$-in) in diameter and 6–7.5-cm ($2\frac{1}{2}$–3-in) long. Insert a cocktail stick (toothpick) through the centre of the tube and leave to dry on a piece of foam sponge.

3 Roll some moulding paste into three cords, 5-cm (2-in) longer than the tube and 3–6-mm ($\frac{1}{8}$–$\frac{1}{4}$-in) thick. Curve the middle of each cord, curl both ends and attach to the sides of the tube, leaving a small space at the top and bottom edges. Leave to dry.

4 When dry, assemble the stand. Attach the cupped petunia shape to the top of the tube with royal icing. Attach the small petunia shape to the larger flat one and secure the tube to this base with royal icing. When dry, paint with non-edible gold colouring.

Flower stand

1 Decorate the basic stand with a garland of tiny plunger-cut flowers made from pink-coloured flower paste (*see page 9*) and attached with royal icing. Pipe dots of royal icing in the centre of each flower.

Flat stand

1 Roll out a long thick cord of moulding paste (*see page 8*) and trim the two ends so as to make a neat join. Stick the ends together to form a circular or oval ring.

2 Attach two rows of frills to the circle or oval, making sure they conceal it completely. Attach to a board covered with sugarpaste. Once dry, dust with petal dust.

Rose stand

1 Roll out some white flower paste (*see page 9*) as thinly as possible. Using a large rose petal cutter, cut out seven petals. Soften the edges with a ball tool and cup each petal. Then curl back the edge of the petal to give it greater realism.

2 Roll out a long cord of flower paste and form it into a ring. Then cut out a circle of thinly rolled paste and attach it to the ring, cupping the centre of the circle.

3 Attach the petals to the circle, overlapping each one slightly. Cut out a further five petals. Soften the edges, cup and curl back the edges as previously. Assemble over the first layer.

4 Using a large rose leaf cutter, cut out five leaves in green-coloured flower paste. Mark the veins with a rose leaf veiner and soften the edges with a ball tool. Cut out three more leaves, using a size smaller cutter and treat in the same way.

5 To assemble the stand, roll out an oval piece of paste 6-mm ($\frac{1}{4}$-in) thick. Attach the five large leaves, so that they cover the paste. Then arrange the smaller leaves on top. Attach the leaf-covered plaque to a round board covered with sugarpaste. Finally attach the assembled rose on top of the leaves. Petal dust edge of rose.

PANSY EGG

1 You will need about 12 pansies to make this egg.
For the calyxes, make small cones of green-coloured flower paste (*see page 9*). Flatten the thick ends to form the shape of Mexican hats. Roll out the flattened parts with a knitting needle until the paste is very thin. Then place a calyx cutter over the top of each cone and press down, turning clockwise. Soften the cut edges with a ball tool.

For the flowers, roll out some yellow-coloured flower paste as thinly as possible and using templates, cut out two back petals and two side petals. Soften the cut edges with a ball tool, frill slightly and cup each petal. Make one base petal in the same way using purple-coloured flower paste.

Moisten the calyx with egg white and attach the two back petals, the second overlapping the first by about one-third. Then attach the two side petals, overlapping the back petals. Place the base petal in position between the side petals.

2 Place a pansy face down in an egg mould, lightly dusted with cornflour (cornstarch). Join a second pansy to the first by moistening the edges of the petals with egg white. Continue adding pansies in this way until the mould is covered, leaving only small spaces between the flowers.

Roll out a long strip of paste about 5-mm ($\frac{1}{4}$-in) wide and 3-mm ($\frac{1}{8}$-in) thick and stick this to the edge of the mould. Leave to dry.

To make the bottom half of the egg, roll out some paste about 3-mm ($\frac{1}{8}$-in) thick and ease into the mould, lightly dusted with cornflour. Make sure that the paste will not stick to the mould by tipping it out and then replacing it. Trim the edge and leave to dry.

To assemble the egg, pipe a line of royal icing on one half and stick the two halves together. Leave to dry. Cover the join with either a row of piped shells or with a ribbon. Paint the details on the base and side petals of each pansy.

3 To make the stand, roll out a long sausage shape of paste. Trim both ends with a sharp knife so that they can be joined neatly. Moisten with egg white and form into an oval. Make two frills and use, one on top of the other, to cover the oval completely.

Attach the egg to the stand with dots of royal icing.

4 Make the butterfly as described on page 20 and position on the top of the egg.

EGG CARD

1 Roll out some moulding paste (*see page 8*) about 3-mm (⅛-in) thick. Cut out two identical rectangles about 18 × 14-cm (7 × 5½-in) for the card. Make two small holes about 4-cm (1½-in) apart and 12-mm (½-in) from the edge of one long side of each rectangle, taking care that the holes are correctly aligned.

2 Make half an egg in white moulding paste in a 7.5-cm (3-in) mould. Leave to dry. Scribe the design on to the outside of the egg. Paint the flower and leaves with food colouring. Then using similarly coloured flower paste, give depth to the design with raised flower work (*see page 39*).

3 Repeat the flower and leaf design in the corner of the front of the card.

4 Position the decorated egg just above the centre of the front of the card and attach with royal icing. Pipe a shell border over the join. Attach some narrow pink satin ribbon around the base of the egg and finish with a bow at the top.
 Make a butterfly (*see page 20*) and attach to the corner of the front of the card. Thread a narrow pink satin ribbon through the holes and tie the two parts of the card together with a double bow.

BUTTERFLY EGG

1 Make an egg in black-coloured moulding paste (*see page 11*) in 14-cm (5½-in) moulds. Leave to dry completely before joining the two halves together with royal icing. If the egg is to be used for purely decorative purposes, it can be sprayed with black car paint when dry (*see page 47*). Otherwise use confectioner's glaze.

2 Either make templates from the patterns of different butterfly wings or use butterfly cutters. Roll out the pastillage gum (*see page 9*) quite thinly cut out two mirror-image wings for each species of butterfly. Soften the edges of the wings with a ball tool. Leave to dry and then paint the wings with food colouring, using a reference book for accuracy.

3 To assemble the butterflies, pipe the bodies in white royal icing on the top of the egg and before they dry, insert the wings, supporting these with small pieces of foam sponge. Use two small headed stamens for the antennae and leave to dry. Then paint the butterfly bodies.

4 Roll some black-coloured moulding paste into a sausage shape and form into a ring. Surround with a frill and position the egg on top. Place on a round board covered with black-coloured moulding paste.

5 Cover the line where the two halves of the egg join with another frill and attach fused black pearls above it, as shown. Attach the butterflies to the egg.

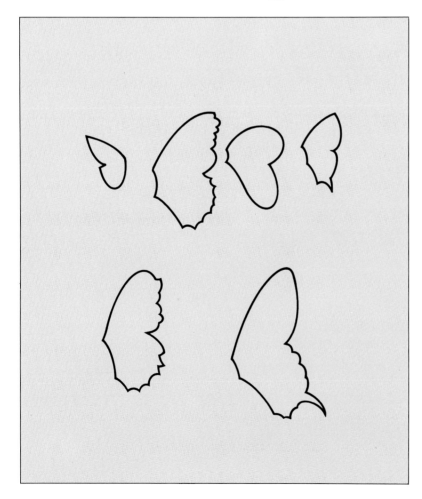

RABBIT EGG

1 Make a pink-coloured caster sugar egg and cut a window in one half (*see page 10*). When dry, stick the two halves together with royal icing.

2 Mould the parts of the rabbit figure, as shown, in white pastillage gum (*see page 9*). Leave to dry and then using a paintbrush and food colourings, add the details. Also mould some flowers and paint in the same way.

3 Attach the rabbit to a small round piece of moulding paste and position inside the egg with the moulded flowers slightly behind the figure.

4 Pipe a row of reverse shells in pink-coloured royal icing around the window and a row of shells around the join.

5 To make the small stand, pack some pink-coloured caster sugar mixture into a 10-cm (4-in) round container. Turn it out. Using a round cutter about 5-cm (2-in) in diameter, cut a hole in the centre and leave to dry. When dry, remove the inner circle and use a little royal icing to attach a piece of gathered lacelon to the ring.

6 Stand the egg in a pink-coloured paste frill and attach to the covered ring. Position on a board covered with white royal icing.

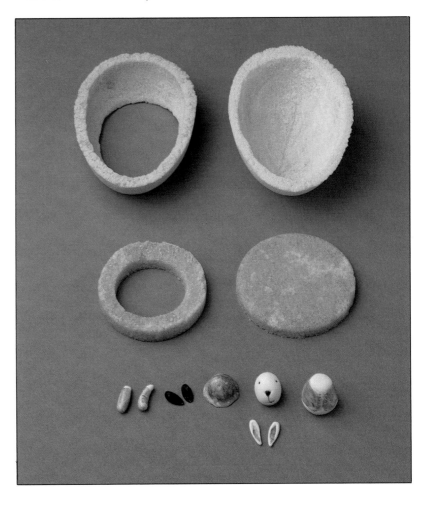

EGGS FOR THE FOUR SEASONS

The four eggs can be grouped together as a table centrepiece to represent the four seasons, or just the appropriate one made at the relevant time of the year.

1 Make the eggs in white moulding paste (*see page 11*). Leave to dry. Either stick the two halves of each egg together or make them into boxes by adding collars to the base halves. The boxes can be lined (*see page 47*).

2 To make a collar, roll out a strip of moulding paste about 6-mm ($\frac{1}{4}$-in) wide and long enough to fit round the egg. Stick the strip to the inside edge of the base, making sure that half the width of the strip is above the top edge of the egg. Leave to dry completely. Check that the top half fits neatly by placing it in position.

3 Invert the top half of the egg and balance over a jam jar. Pipe a shell border on the edge, making sure that half is piped below the edge of the egg. Leave to dry. The shell border will help to conceal the line where the two halves join.

4 Attach narrow satin ribbon in the appropriate colour above the shell border and narrow green satin ribbon round the edge of each base egg.

5 Mould appropriate flowers for each season – for example, primroses, violets and primrose leaves for spring; roses, forget-me-nots and rose leaves for summer; chrysanthemums and leaves for autumn; and holly and berries for winter.
  If the flowers are wired into a spray, make a hole in the top of the egg with a craft knife and push the wire through. Alternatively, the flowers can be attached to the egg with royal icing.

CASTER SUGAR EGG WITH MOULDED FLOWERS

1 Make an egg in caster sugar mixture (*see page 10*). Leave to dry. Join the two halves and cover the line with a shell border in yellow-coloured royal icing.

2 Make the plaque in a petal-shaped chocolate mould or box. Leave to dry. Position the egg at a slight angle.

3 Use flower paste (*see page 9*) to mould about fifteen daisies, a few chrysanthemum leaves and 30–40 ivy leaves in different sizes.

4 Wire the ivy leaves together and curve to the shape of the egg, as shown. Arrange the daisies and chrysanthemum leaves in a small pieces of paste and attach the wired ivy leaves. Use royal icing at intervals to hold the spray firmly in position on the egg.

CHOCOLATE EGG

1 Make a chocolate egg in patterned moulds. Leave to dry. Join the two halves with melted chocolate and attach to a round silver board with a little melted chocolate.

2 Make a frill in moulding chocolate (made by adding liquid glucose to the melted chocolate) and position around the base of the egg.

3 Cover the line where the two halves join with a shell border in pale yellow-coloured royal icing.

4 Mould one open yellow rose in flower paste (*see page 9*) and dust the edges of the petals with pink dusting powder. Then make a yellow-coloured rose bud and five green-coloured rose leaves in flower paste. Arrange the rose and leaves on top of the egg, attaching with a little royal icing.

REVERSE CUT EGG

1 Make an egg in white moulding paste (*see page 8*). Make a template from the pattern in thin card and place inside one half, pressing firmly with the fingertips of one hand. Using a scalpel or craft knife, cut round the outline and leaves in the mould to dry.

2 When dry, remove the cut-out egg shape and set aside. Stick the two halves together with royal icing. Invert the cut-out egg shape and surround with two rows of frills to cover the cut edge.

3 Pipe a thick shell border in royal icing round the cut edge of the top half of the egg and attach the cut-out shape. Dust the inside of this with twinkle-pink dusting powder.

4 Mould the cupid in white pastillage gum (*see page 9*), dust with silver snowflake dusting powder and attach to the inside of the cut-out egg shape.

5 Cover the line where the two halves join with pink satin ribbon and fused pearls. Using narrower pink satin ribbon and fused pearls, frame the inside of the cut-out shape in the same way. Position the egg on a decorative gold-coloured stand.

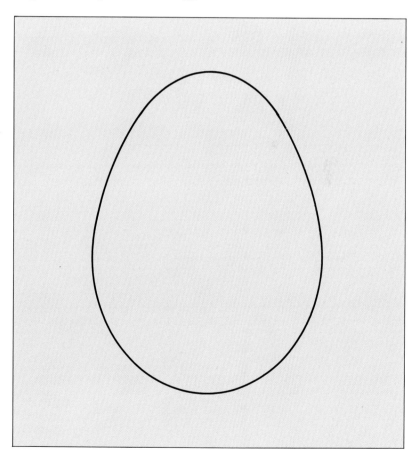

FABERGÉ NEST EGG

1 Make the first egg in deep burgundy-coloured moulding paste (*see page 8*) in 19-cm (7½-in) moulds. To make the burgundy colour, mix claret and red colourings with a tiny amount of black paste. Make the second egg in off-white-coloured moulding paste in 14-cm (5½-in) moulds. Make the third egg in white moulding paste in 7.5-cm (3-in) moulds: when dry, paint this one with gold food colouring.

2 Make colours for the bases of each egg to form boxes. Roll out three strips of moulding paste about 6-mm (¼-in) wide. Attach one to the inside edge of each base with a little royal icing, making sure that half the width of the strip is above the edge of the egg.

3 Mould a baby chicken in pastillage gum paste (*see page* 9). When dry, paint with gold food colouring and place inside the golden egg.

4 Make a template from the design and scribe the outline on the burgundy- and off-white-coloured eggs. For the burgundy-coloured eggs, use cream-coloured royal icing for the brush embroidery and for the off-white one, burgundy-coloured royal icing. Leave to dry completely before fitting the eggs inside each other.

5 Make a round plaque with a scalloped edge in cream-coloured moulding paste and repeat the brush embroidery floral design in burgundy-coloured royal icing. Position the egg in the centre of the plaque.

CHRISTENING EGG

1 Make an egg in white moulding paste (*see page 11*), moulding one half on the inside of the mould and the other on the outside. When dry, attach the former to the inside of the latter in an upright position, as shown. Dust the inside of the egg with pink or blue dusting powder depending on whether the baby is a girl or a boy.

2 Attach one frill slightly below the edge of the horizontal egg and another just on the inside edge to cover it. Then attach a frill to the inside edge of the upright egg, easing it back as shown. Cover the join inside the upright egg with narrow pink satin ribbon and tie a bow at the top. Also cover the join at the back of the upright egg with ribbon.

3 Use a baby mould to make the figure in pastillage gum (*see page 9*). When dry, paint the facial features. Make the mattress from a rectangle of pastillage, about 6-mm ($\frac{1}{4}$-in) thick, dried over a curved shape. Use a smaller rectangle of pastillage for the pillow, thin the edges and frill with a cocktail stick (toothpick). Press the baby's head when dry on the pillow to dent it, as shown. Roll another rectangle of pastillage out quite thinly for the blanket and frill the edge. Lay over the cradle and fold the top edge over.

4 Attach the cradle to an oval piece of moulding paste and position on a round board covered with royal icing. Pipe the baby's name in the appropriate-coloured royal icing.

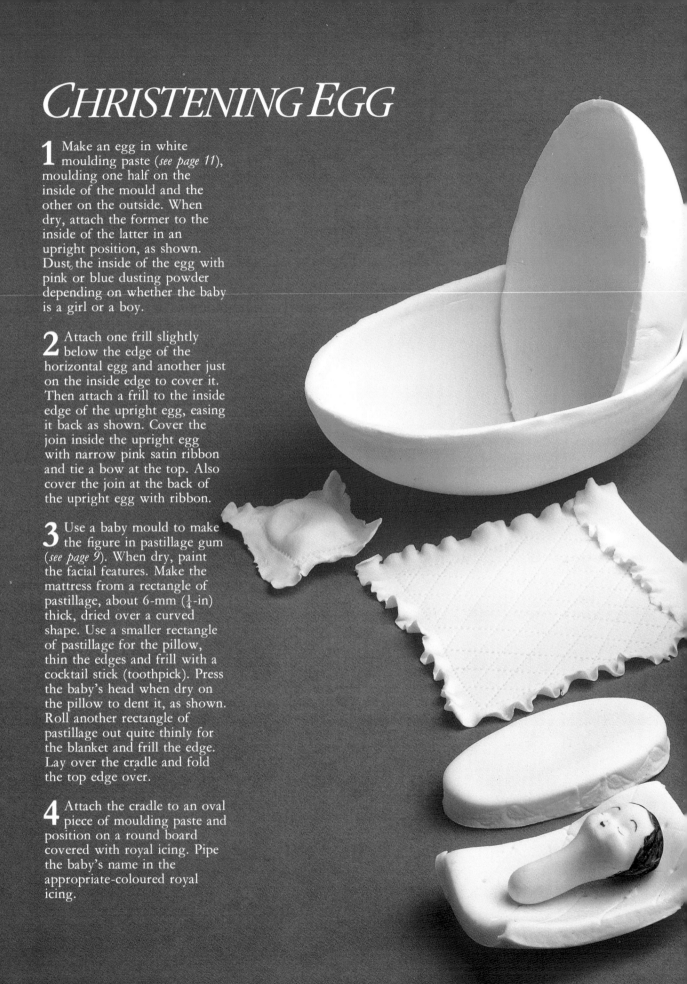

HOUSEWARMING EGG

1 Make an egg in moulding paste (*see page 11*). Make a template from the pattern and cut a door in the lower part of one half (*see page 11*). Leave to dry. Paint the egg quite roughly with brown food colouring.

2 Make two pictures from tiny rectangles of paste and paint as liked. Attach these to the back of the inside of the half of the egg without a door opening. Fit a flat round piece of paste in the base of the same half to form the floor.

Roll out a small rectangle of paste, fringe both ends and paint with a suitable design for the rug. Arrange some dolls' furniture on the rug, securing with a little royal icing. Leave to dry before attaching the other half of the egg with royal icing.

3 Paint the bottom half of the egg to resemble a brick wall.

To make the roof, roll out a strip of moulding paste, scallop one edge and attach to the egg at an angle with royal icing.

Pipe lines of straw-coloured royal icing below the scalloped strip and then cover it with more lines to make the thatched roof. Cut another scalloped strip and attach it, slightly overlapping the first. Pipe more lines of straw-coloured royal icing. Continue in this way until the top of the egg is completely covered. Attach a silver-coloured chimney on one side of the roof.

4 Position the egg in a stand made from a circle of moulding paste covered with a slightly smaller ring. Attach to the prepared board which has been covered in paste with green-coloured royal icing roughed up to resemble grass. Make some pebbles in

moulding paste and attach to the grass.

5 Make the steps, shutters, windows and window-box in moulding paste. Leave to dry and attach to the house with royal icing. Paint in bright colours, as shown.

6 Pipe a climbing plant around the house. Make two plant pots in moulding paste and fill with piped flowers, using green- and pink-coloured royal icing.

7 Make a small plaque and pipe the inscription. Attach to a small post made in moulding paste. Finally position a little mouse, made in moulding paste and then painted, on the front step.

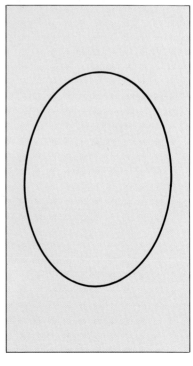

VALENTINE EGG

1 Make an egg in pale pink-coloured moulding paste (*see page 11*). Make a template from the heart-shaped pattern and use to make a door in one half of the egg (*see page 11*). Leave to dry for 6–8 hours.

2 When the egg is firm enough to hold its shape, remove from the mould and insert pieces of narrow pink satin ribbon to outline the heart-shaped door. Pipe a shell border around the edge, as shown. Leave to dry completely before joining the two halves with royal icing. Decorate the top of the egg with a spray of moulded bleeding hearts and leaves.

3 For the larger stand, roll out some moulding paste about 6-mm ($\frac{1}{4}$-in) thick and cut out a heart shape. Crimp the edge and insert narrow pink satin ribbon, as shown.

4 Use a fluted heart-shaped mould for the smaller stand, cupping the top for the egg. Attach pieces of narrow pink satin ribbon in the grooves, as shown. Position the egg in the cupped top of the stand, attaching with royal icing. Place the larger stand on a silver heart-shaped board. Finally cover the line where the eggs are joined with lace-work in pale pink-coloured royal icing.

If liked, you can tuck a tiny bunch of roses inside the egg and make a heart-shaped gift tag with the recipient's name.

RAISED FLOWER EGG

1 Make an egg in moulding paste (*see page 11*). Leave to dry. Join the two halves together and cover the line with two frills, one curling slightly upwards and the other slightly downwards. Attach a length of fused pearls between the frills.

2 Make a template from the pattern of the floral design and scribe the outline on to the top half of the egg. Paint the background in appropriate food colourings. Then paint the flowers and leaves as outlined.

3 Either make templates for the individual petals or use a flower cutter. Cut out the different petals in thinly rolled flower paste (*see page 9*), appropriately coloured. Two back petals, four side petals and three base petals are needed for each flower.

Smooth the edges of the petals with a ball tool and cup the undersides.

Using the tip of a Dresden tool and a little egg white, attach each petal by its point in sequence: firstly, the two back petals (marked 'A') slightly overlapping each other, then the two side petals (marked 'B') and finally the base petal (marked 'C').

Attach another side petal over each of the original ones and two more petals over the original base one to create the raised flower effect.

Make one bud with a green-coloured calyx for the top left-hand side of the design, as shown.

Paint the stems, the veining on the leaves, and shading and stamens on the petals in appropriate food colourings.

Position the egg on a decorative metal stand.

39

CASTER SUGAR EGG WITH BAS RELIEF

1 Make an egg in caster sugar mixture (*see page 10*).

2 Paint the sky and ground on one half of the egg with appropriate food colourings.

3 To make the bas relief for the bears, roll out a piece of sugarpaste about 3-mm ($\frac{1}{8}$-in) thick. Make a template from the pattern and cut out the design. Smooth the edge with your fingertips to give it a rounded finish. Lay the design over the painted half of the egg and tuck tiny pieces of paste under the parts that should be given greater depth, such as the head and arms.

   Cut round the arms with a scalpel or craft knife and, using a Dresden tool, press the surrounding areas so that the arms come forward. Work over the whole design in this way, working quite fast so that the paste does not dry out. When dry, paint in appropriate colours.

4 Join the two halves together with royal icing and cover the line with a shell border.

5 Make a circular caster sugar plaque (*see page 23*) and a slightly smaller ring for the stand. Position the egg in the ring at an angle, as shown. Surround with white lace and display on a round board covered with sugarpaste.

CASTER SUGAR EGG WITH PIPED FLOWERS

1 Make an egg in caster sugar mixture (*see page 10*). Leave to dry. Join the two halves with royal icing and cover the line with a shell border in pale yellow-coloured royal icing.

Make a plaque in the lid of a heart-shaped sweet box and a small circular stand in caster sugar mixture.

2 Pipe eight pansies in yellow-coloured royal icing and leave to dry on waxed paper or plastic wrap.

3 Attach the pansies to the front of the egg and paint the details on the petals with food colourings. Pipe the stems and leaves in green-coloured royal icing directly on to the egg to make an attractive arrangement.

4 Attach the egg to the small stand and position on the heart-shaped plaque.

MINIATURE CHRISTMAS EGGS

1 Roll some moulding paste (*see page 8*) into a long sausage shape. Cut into tiny, equal-sized pieces and shape each one into an egg. Make a hole for the cords by inserting a long hat pin or a clean nail through each egg. Leave to dry.

2 When dry, paint the eggs with Christmas motifs or stick small blossoms and leaves on the eggs.

3 Fold 10-cm (4-in) lengths of gold cord in half and thread the folded ends through the eggs, tying a knot at the other ends. These miniature eggs can be hung on a Christmas tree or used as an unusual centrepiece on your Christmas table.

CANDY BOX

1 Make an egg in moulding paste (*see page 11*) in 19-cm (7½-in) moulds. Either use coloured paste or paint the box when dry. As the box shown is not intended to be edible, it was sprayed with a deep blue car paint which gives the egg a rich colour.

Make sure that the two halves are completely dry before colouring them in this way. Invert each half over a jam jar and stand these in a large cardboard box, so that the surrounding area is not covered with paint too. Leave to dry for about 2 hours and repeat with two more coats of paint. Then turn the eggs over and repeat the process on the inside, especially on the edges.

2 Make a collar (*see page 24*) in moulding paste and when dry paint gold. Attach to the base of the egg.

3 Attach gold braid around the outside edge of the lid. A decorative drawer knob is used for the handle. Make a hole in the centre of the lid with a pin and press the knob into position gently.

4 Cut two oval shapes about 4-cm (1½-in) larger than the egg in any suitable material to line the egg. Stick the edge of the material to the edge of each half, gathering it in soft folds. Cover the join with narrow gold braid.

5 Fill the base of the egg with foil-wrapped miniature eggs. Position the egg on a gold-coloured metal stand.

EGGS AS FAVOURS

1 Make eggs in caster sugar mixture (*see page 8*) in 5-cm (2-in) moulds.

2 For a children's party, join the two halves together and cover the line with a shell border in appropriately coloured royal icing.

Dust the eggs with shimmering dusting powder in different colours. Either pipe the names of the children or figure pipe rabbits or teddy bears in royal icing on the eggs.

3 For a wedding, do not join the two halves together. Decorate the top halves of the eggs with plunger-cut flowers and piped leaves. Place a few sugared almonds in the bottom halves.

Use moulding paste (*see page 8*) to make little heart-shaped tags. Cut a hole at the top and pipe the date and initials of the bride and groom in royal icing. Wrap narrow satin ribbon around the two halves of each egg, threading one end through the tag, and finish with a neat bow.

BIRTHDAY EGG

1 Make an egg in white moulding paste (*see page 8*). Finish drying one half on its curved side rather than inverted so as to obtain a small flattened area for the base. When completely dry, stick the two halves together with royal icing.

2 Make twelve toy soldiers in a mould. Either leave to dry over a curved former or attach them to the egg immediately so that they dry in a curved shape. When dry, paint the soldiers' uniforms and their facial features.

3 Pipe the child's name in red-coloured royal icing on the top of the egg. Position the egg on a round board covered with white moulding paste.

MARBLED EGGS

1 Colour small quantities of marzipan different shades, adding the appropriate flavourings. For example, use oil of violet for violet-coloured marzipan, peppermint for green-coloured marzipan, orange for orange-coloured marzipan, strawberry for pink-coloured marzipan and brandy for brown-coloured marzipan.

2 Use an equal amount of coloured and white marzipan for each egg and mix together lightly to create a marbled effect. Form into egg shapes and leave to dry.

3 Arrange the marbled eggs in a basket.

GOOSE EGGS

The elaborately decorated eggs shown in the photograph were all made from goose eggs. They exemplify the versatility of the egg shape and explore the potential of using real eggs for more permanent decorations.

The cut-out egg with the swans was made for a silver wedding and the three-part egg with the cupid to celebrate a golden wedding.

Probably the most famous decorated eggs are those created by Carl Fabergé, who was the favourite jeweller of the Russian Imperial family, the Romanovs. Between 1884 and 1917 he created beautiful eggs from percious metals and gems which the Czar and his family would give to one another as presents at Easter and on other special occasions.

These eggs were not only exquisite but ingenious as well. Concealed amongst the jewels were tiny springs which released surprises from within the eggs. Little clocks, jewel-encrusted birds and tiny replicas of the Imperial family would be revealed when the secret spring was discovered. This idea was adopted by the Victorians who liked to place little surprises, such as miniature sewing kits or musical boxes, in fancy eggs.

The two most famous collections of Fabergé's work in existence today are housed in the Forbes Collection; New York and the Armoury in Moscow.

The Russians have a long tradition of giving eggs as Easter gifts, ranging from the jewelled eggs given by the aristocracy, marble or jade eggs which wealthy ladies would use to keep their hands cool, to the brightly painted wooden eggs given by the poorer people. Wooden nest-eggs were popular, the layers of which could be unscrewed to reveal increasingly smaller eggs inside, similar to the famous Russian *matrioska* dolls.

Today, people collect eggs of many types, some specializing in one particular kind, such as marble eggs. Many enthusiasts collect shell eggs which can be found decorated in many beautiful and interesting ways, for example hand-painted egg shells, or shells decorated with filigree or *découpage* work.

Strangely, there does not appear to be a name for people who collect eggs. There is one, however, for collections of egg cups – *pocillovi*, a word of Italian origin.

COLLECTING DECORATIVE EGGS

In the different countries of the world decorative eggs have been made in almost every known medium from precious metals to wood.

The egg on the stand comes from India. The designs on the two shell eggs, threaded with ribbons, were created with onion skins, a popular custom in the rural areas of England in the last century. The red egg is marble and the white one alabaster. The others are wooden, painted with intricate Oriental designs.

A collection of varied types of fancy eggs is an invaluable source of inspiration to the creative sugarcraft artist.

Real eggs need to be blown, sterilized and strengthened before they can be decorated, and the following instructions apply not only to goose eggs but to any other kind of shell egg being prepared for decoration. Pierce a hole in both ends of the egg. A hobby drill will give the neatest results but if one is not available, a darning needle may be used. Insert a cocktail stick (toothpick) and move it about to break up the yolk.

Traditionally, eggs were blown by placing the mouth over one of the holes and blowing the contents out through the other. However, it is more hygienic to blow through a short piece of drinking straw or to use an empty washing-up liquid container and puff air through the nozzle by squeezing. Once all the contents have been removed, sterilize the egg by dipping it in a disinfectant solution. Leave it to dry for two days. Once dry, strengthen the egg by painting with five coats of paint.

To make windows in a painted egg, cut out a template of the required shape and mark the outline in pencil on to the eggshell. Drill around the outline with a hobby drill. Once you have gained access to the inside of the egg, it may be necessary to clean it with a damp cottonwool bud before decorating it.

To make a casket, use a hacksaw blade to cut the egg in half. Clean the inside, then the egg is ready to be lined and decorated.

If you want to make a hinged casket, first make a small cut of about the same size as the hinge with a hacksaw blade. Attach the hinge to the outside of the egg with clear glue, taking care to avoid the pin. Leave to dry and then cut through the remaining shell neatly.

NOVELTY EGGS

The egg shape lends itself perfectly to transformation into a variety of amusing and imaginative figures for children's parties, providing the perfect base for painted and decorated faces. The photographs show just a few examples of the many attractive items that can easily be made, including a punk family and different kinds of stylized animals and birds.

Find inspiration from children's books, comics and toys, or have fun decorating the eggs to look like favourite television personalities or characters from the worlds of film or pantomime. A delightful and unusual idea for a small party is to make an egg to resemble each of the guests and put them around the table with place-name cards.

Either make the basic egg shapes using moulding paste or buy sugar-coated chocolate eggs. Paint the nose, eyes and mouth on to the egg or, for a more realistic effect, use moulding or flower paste (*see page 9*) to make the different features and attach them to the egg with royal icing

or egg white. Paint on some rosy cheeks. The hair and moustaches, beards and eyebrows can be painted on or moulded individually in paste and then attached. Set the heads on 'necks' made from moulding paste and place them on stands.

Then decorate the figures with collars, bow-ties, scarves and other colourful accessories. Hats add character to the figures, as shown in the photograph opposite by the woman's red hat with a white band and the man's jaunty black bowler. Hats can be modelled in paste and attached to the egg securely with royal icing or egg white.

Real eggs can also be used as a base for novelty figures. Blow, sterilize and paint the eggs as described on page 54. As these eggs are not edible, there are many different paints to choose from. Car spray or pearlized paint gives an excellent finish. If you use a water-based paint, it is necessary to apply a top coat of gloss varnish to seal it.

Once the paint is completely dry, paint on features and attach hair and accessories with glue.

FISH & SWAN EGGS

The stylized fish and graceful swan shown in the photographs opposite and above are attractively displayed on plaques made of sugarpaste, which have decorative scalloped edges.

Bought eggs have been used for the bodies of both fish and swan and in the photographs you can see the individual features which are made separately in moulding paste and then attached to the eggs with royal icing or egg white.

To make the stylized fish it is necessary to make the tail, fins, scales, mouth and base in pinky-orange-coloured moulding paste, then score the fins and tail to give a ridged impression. Attach the scales to the body first, using egg white or royal icing, arranging them carefully in overlapping rows, as shown. Attach the fins and the tail. Make eyes in moulding paste and attach these to the fish.

An effective way of giving the impression that the fish is surrounded by water is to make some greeny-blue-coloured jelly, leave to set, then chop it up and arrange it on the plaque around the base of the fish.

The swan will need two wings, a tail and a curved head/neck piece moulded in white moulding paste. Feather the edges of the wings and tail for a more realistic appearance. With red-coloured moulding paste, shape the feet and beak and attach the beak to the head. Assemble the swan using royal icing or egg white. Obviously, this method can be adapted to create other birds – look through reference books for inspiration – but the swan is certainly one of the most effective shapes.

RABBIT EGG

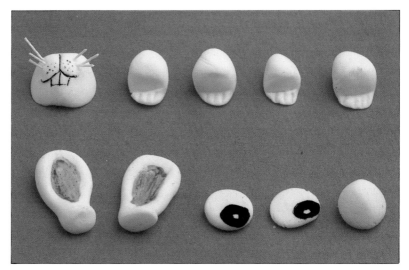

This humorous novelty rabbit is always a favourite at children's parties or as a decoration for Easter.

A bought egg has been used to make the body, set on a sugarpaste plaque with a scalloped edge. The features have been moulded in moulding paste and attached to the rabbit's body with royal icing or egg white.

The photograph above shows the individually moulded pieces. You will need to make a nose and mouth piece, marking in the outline of the mouth and teeth and using cotton stamens for the whiskers. Make four paws from balls of moulding paste, flattening and scoring one side of each ball to represent the 'toes'. Make the ears, colouring the insides pink, the eyes and, finally, a ball of moulding paste for the tail. Assemble the rabbit using royal icing or egg white and attach it to the plaque with a disc of moulding paste to give it a firm base.

The rabbit shown here has been decorated with pretty pink fabric flowers stuck between her ears. There are, of course, many other decorative possibilities. Why not make a family of rabbits for Easter, using smaller eggs for the bodies of the young ones, dressed up in their Easter bonnets which can be moulded in coloured paste.

PIG EGG

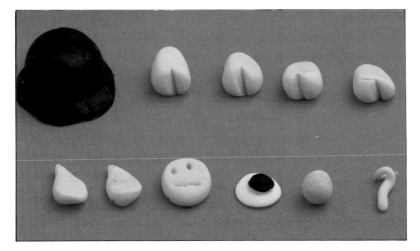

Pigs are very popular forms of decoration at children's parties or as novelty gifts. They can either be modelled realistically, made in a stylized form or created as crazy caricatures with exaggerated features and funny hats and accessories.

The amusing pig characters pictured opposite have been made using bought eggs for the bodies. The photograph above shows the individual pieces which can be made from moulding paste (*see page 9*) and attached to the body with either royal icing or egg white.

For each pig, using pink-coloured moulding paste, model four legs, making a deep indent in the base of each to represent the trotter. Mould the ears, which can be attached to the bodies at varying angles to give more expression. Make the snout from a flattened ball of paste, indenting holes for the nose and a line for the mouth. White and black-coloured paste is used to create the eyes and, finally, mould a thin, curly tail from pink-coloured paste. Attach all the individual pieces to the pigs with royal icing or egg white. Dress Mr and Mrs Pig in fancy hats, as shown in the photograph, modelled in coloured moulding or flower paste.

The instructions given for these pigs can easily be adapted to make other farm animals such as cows and sheep, and smaller eggs can be used to make piglets, calves and lambs to accompany them. Children's books and toys should provide some further helpful ideas for creating animal caricatures.

A bought egg is used is used for
the clown's head. His frill and
cheeks are dusted with pink
dusting powder.